THE HORROR OF
WORLD WAR II

by Nancy Dickmann

Consultant: Philip Parker
Author and historian

capstone

Infosearch books are published by Capstone Press,
1710 Roe Crest Drive, North Mankato, Minnesota 56003
www.mycapstone.com

Library of Congress Cataloging-in-Publication Data
Library of Congress Cataloging-in-Publication data is available on the Library of Congress website.

978-1-4846-4165-1 (library binding)
978-1-4846-4169-9 (paperback)
978-1-4846-4173-6 (eBook PDF)

Editorial Credits
Editor: Nancy Dickmann
Designer: Rocket Design (East Anglia) Ltd
Production Specialist: Kathy McColley
Media Researchers: Nancy Dickmann,
Steve White-Thomson, and Izzi Howell
Illustrators: Rocket Design (East Anglia) Ltd and Ron Dixon

Photo Credits
Alamy: DOD Photo, 43, Everett Collection Historical, 6, 38, Granger Historical Picture Archive, 29, 30, Nordicphotos, 28, Paul Broadbent, 33, RGB Ventures/SuperStock, 15, World History Archive, 34, 40, 42, Shutterstock: Aksenenko Olga, 3 (dirt), 44 (dirt), Aleksandra Pikalova, 3 (grenade), chrisdorney, 26, Edvard Molnar, 25 (soldier silhouette), Elzbieta Sekowska, 8, Everett Historical, 1, 4, 5, 7, 9, 11, 12, 14, 18, 20, 24, 25, 27, 31, 32, 35, 36, 37, 41, Jorg Hackemann, 17, LandFox, 16, Leonard Zhukovsky, 23, Martial Red, 7 (skull and crossbones), Oliver Denker, 13, pkorchagina, 19, Tshooter, 15 (warship outlines), SuperStock: cover, Fototeca Gilardi/Marka, 22.

Printed in the United States of America.
010365F17

Table of Contents

What Was World War II?

The first truly global war lasted from 1914 to 1918. It was long and bloody and involved people from around the world. It was so destructive that many hoped it would be "the war to end wars" — but it wasn't. Just 20 years later, the world was plunged into an even bigger, deadlier war.

In September 1939, Germany invaded Poland. This set off a chain of events that would see dozens of countries pulled into the war. By the end, about 50 to 60 million people were dead. This was about 2.5 percent of the entire world population at the time. Well over half of the deaths were **civilians**, including many children.

■ Millions of civilians were killed or forced from their homes during the war.

TOTAL WAR

Powerful new weapons, such as **atomic bombs**, made WWII extremely deadly. But this wasn't just a war fought by soldiers. Civilians were deeply involved as well. Some made weapons and **ammunition**, while others filled in for workers who were away fighting. This involvement made them targets. Some were forced to work and others were killed outright. Bombing raids on cities targeted all civilians living there, not just those working for the war effort. Millions of people suffered food shortages as a result of the war.

◼ **The fighting left roads and towns in ruins, making life difficult.**

How Did the War Start?

World War II had its roots in World War I. In 1918, Germany and its allies had been defeated by a coalition of France, Russia, the United Kingdom, and the United States. After the war, the losers were treated harshly. Germany had to pay huge amounts of **compensation** to other countries. It lost some of its territory, and its military was restricted.

■ After WWI, **inflation** in Germany spiraled out of control. Money became so worthless that some people burned it for fuel.

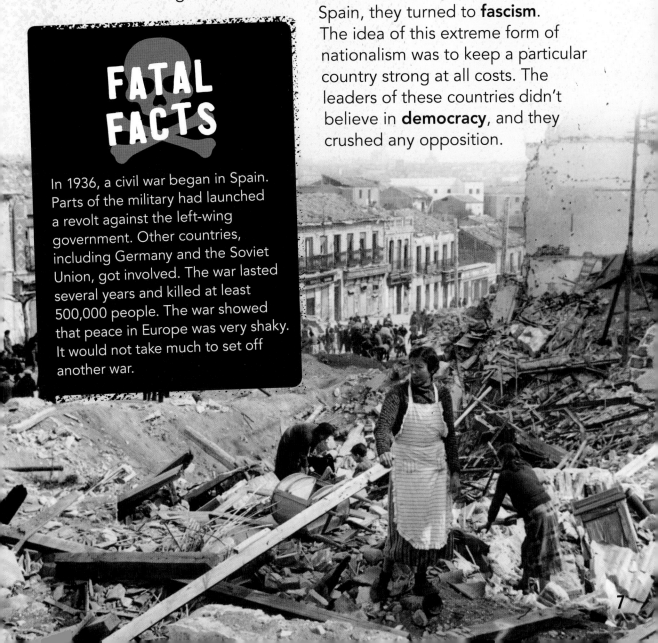

A WORLD IN TURMOIL

The war had left the economies of many countries in ruins. A worldwide **depression** soon followed. In some countries, huge numbers of people were out of work and struggling to get by. This caused anger and unrest. People started to look for strong leaders to solve their countries' problems.

In some countries, powerful **dictators** took charge. They promised to make their nation great, no matter what it took. In Italy, Germany, and Spain, they turned to **fascism**. The idea of this extreme form of nationalism was to keep a particular country strong at all costs. The leaders of these countries didn't believe in **democracy**, and they crushed any opposition.

FATAL FACTS

In 1936, a civil war began in Spain. Parts of the military had launched a revolt against the left-wing government. Other countries, including Germany and the Soviet Union, got involved. The war lasted several years and killed at least 500,000 people. The war showed that peace in Europe was very shaky. It would not take much to set off another war.

FASCISM IN GERMANY

In Germany, a WWI veteran named Adolf Hitler was becoming popular. He became leader of the German Workers' Party in 1921. He renamed it the National Socialist German Workers' Party — or the Nazi Party, for short. In 1933, he was named **chancellor** of Germany. He soon had complete control of the country.

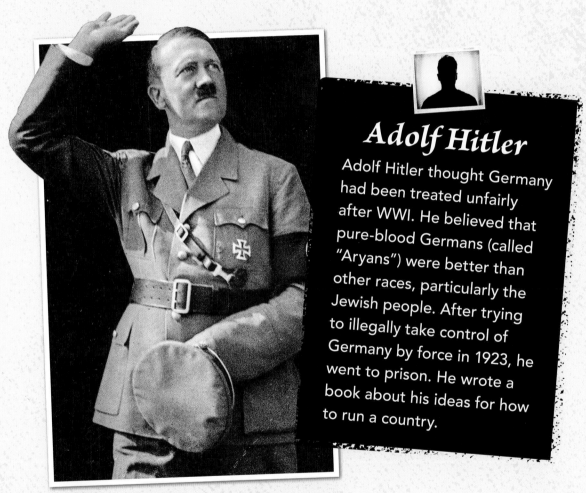

Adolf Hitler

Adolf Hitler thought Germany had been treated unfairly after WWI. He believed that pure-blood Germans (called "Aryans") were better than other races, particularly the Jewish people. After trying to illegally take control of Germany by force in 1923, he went to prison. He wrote a book about his ideas for how to run a country.

TROUBLE IN ASIA

In Asia, Japan's power was growing. It invaded China in 1937. This started a bitter campaign that would leave millions dead. Japan wanted to control East Asia and the Pacific. They signed agreements with Germany and Italy. The three countries promised to help each other out.

THE ROAD TO WAR

Hitler's armies marched into Austria in March 1938. Austria was now part of Germany. Next on Hitler's list of land to take over was the western part of Czechoslovakia, where many Germans lived. British and French leaders met with Hitler in Munich. They agreed to let him take the area. They thought this would prevent war, but they were wrong.

■ Prime Minister Chamberlain returned to London in triumph after signing the Munich Agreement.

HISTORY UNLOCKED

After Munich, Prime Minister Neville Chamberlain spoke to the British people. He said: "For the second time in our history, a British prime minister has returned from Germany bringing peace with honour. I believe it is peace for our time."

Another politician, Winston Churchill, criticized the agreement. He said: "You were given the choice between war and dishonour. You chose dishonour, and you will have war."

Who Took Sides in the War?

It became clear that Hitler was thinking about invading Poland. British and French leaders said that they would help Poland if it was attacked. But Hitler wasn't too worried. He signed a secret agreement with the Soviet Union. It was a promise between the two countries not to go to war with each other. On September 1, 1939, Germany invaded Poland.

LINING UP

Within days, the United Kingdom and France declared war on Germany. Many countries decided to stay **neutral** rather than taking sides. But neutrality didn't always save them from invasion. After eight months with little fighting, the Germans attacked. They took over Norway, Denmark, Luxembourg, Belgium, the Netherlands, and France.

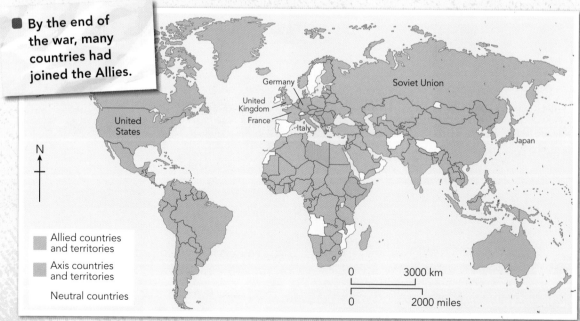

■ By the end of the war, many countries had joined the Allies.

Germany

United Kingdom

France

Italy

Soviet Union

United States

Japan

N

■ Allied countries and territories

■ Axis countries and territories

Neutral countries

0   3000 km

0   2000 miles

The two sides became known as the "Axis" and the "Allies." Germany, Italy, and Japan made up the Axis. They were later joined by other Eastern European countries. After France fell, the main Allies were the United Kingdom and China. They were joined by the Soviet Union in June 1941.

THE UNITED STATES

The United States was determined to stay out of another bloody European war. However, President Franklin D. Roosevelt was sympathetic to the Allies. He helped his country provide them with weapons and other supplies. Then, on December 7, 1941, the Japanese attacked Hawaii. Their target was the naval base at Pearl Harbor. The United States entered the war the next day.

UNITED we are strong

UNITED we will win

■ Both sides used **propaganda** to affect public opinion.

HISTORY UNLOCKED

Roosevelt gave a speech on December 8, asking Congress to declare war. He said: "There is no blinking at the fact that our people, our territory, and our interests are in grave danger."

What Deadly Weapons Were Used?

Weapons in WWII ranged from traditional to cutting-edge. During the war, engineers raced to come up with bigger and better weapons. Tiny improvements, such as making a plane a bit faster, could make a huge difference. Factories worked around the clock to produce vehicles, weapons, and ammunition. Keeping troops supplied was a huge job.

GUNS AND ARTILLERY

Most foot soldiers carried weapons such as pistols, rifles, and grenades. These weapons had been around since the last war, but the newer models were more efficient and reliable. Armies also depended on **artillery**. These large guns shot explosive shells over long distances. They could be used to destroy enemy defenses before an attack.

With so many men away fighting, women were hired to produce weapons.

TANK WARFARE

Tanks made their first appearance in World War I. By the 1930s, they had improved enormously. They played a much larger role in WWII. Tanks had heavy, powerful guns that could inflict a lot of damage. Their caterpillar tracks let them be driven almost anywhere.

American soldiers used a new weapon, the bazooka, against tanks. This portable rocket launcher could be used by a single soldier. It fired small explosive rockets. They could penetrate through armor about 5 inches (12 centimeters) thick.

FATAL FACTS

Tanks could be death traps. The M4 Sherman tank was one of the main types used during the war, but it had a reputation for catching fire after taking a hit. It was even worse when the fire ignited the ammunition stored inside. Whole crews could be killed this way.

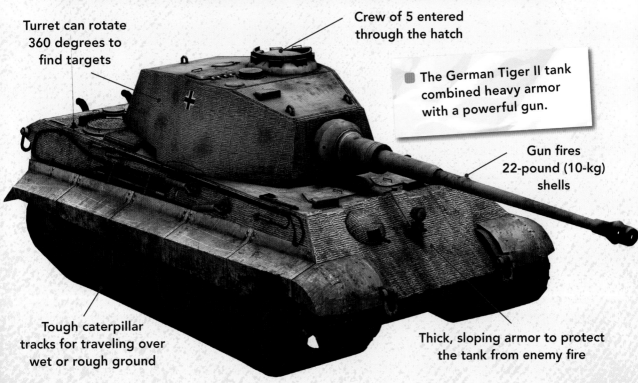

Turret can rotate 360 degrees to find targets

Crew of 5 entered through the hatch

The German Tiger II tank combined heavy armor with a powerful gun.

Gun fires 22-pound (10-kg) shells

Tough caterpillar tracks for traveling over wet or rough ground

Thick, sloping armor to protect the tank from enemy fire

FIGHTING SHIPS

The war was fought at sea as well as on land. Both sides wanted to control the main shipping routes. If they could cut off the enemy's supply lines, it gave them an advantage. Navies used enormous battleships, which were heavily armed. They could hit targets accurately from almost 20 miles (32 kilometers) away. Destroyers were smaller and more nimble. They used **torpedoes** and guns against other ships.

HIDDEN BENEATH THE WAVES

Submarines could launch surprise attacks by approaching from below. The Germans used more submarines than any other country, but nearly 800 of them were sunk. Often the whole crew would be killed. The German submarine service lost 68 percent of its sailors. About 28,000 were killed.

Karl Dönitz

Karl Dönitz had served as an officer on German submarines in World War I. By World War II, he was in charge of Germany's submarine fleet. He developed many of their **tactics**.

German submarines sank about 3,000 Allied ships during the war.

AIRCRAFT CARRIERS

Aircraft carriers let navies launch bombing raids almost anywhere in the world. Planes could take off, land, refuel, and take off again. Aircraft carriers had an advantage over battleships. The planes they launched had greater range than naval guns. They could hit targets more accurately.

Planes on aircraft carriers could fold up their wings to save space.

The United States and Japan were fighting for control of the Pacific Ocean. Their aircraft carriers clashed in several huge battles. The biggest was the Battle of Leyte Gulf in 1944. Australian forces joined the United States to inflict huge losses on the Japanese.

BATTLE OF LEYTE GULF BY THE NUMBERS

		Allied forces	Japanese forces
Aircraft carriers		8	1
Smaller carriers		26	3
Battleships		12	9
Cruisers		24	20
Destroyers		166	35
Airplanes		1,500	300

WARPLANES

Airplanes were a key weapon during the war. Some flew from aircraft carriers. Others operated from airfields on land. Planes could take photos of enemy positions. Fighter planes, such as the British Spitfire, shot down enemy planes. Bombers dropped explosives on troops, factories, and ports.

■ The Hawker Hurricane fighter was used to attack bombers approaching Britain.

BOMBING RAIDS

Both sides launched bombing raids on enemy cities. The biggest type of bomb weighed 11 tons (10,000 kg) and could go through thick concrete. **Incendiary bombs** were designed to start fires. In March 1945, a raid dropped 500,000 incendiary bombs on Toyko. About 100,000 people died.

HISTORY UNLOCKED

French reporter Robert Guillain wrote this after witnessing the **firebombing** of Tokyo.

"As they fell, cylinders scattered a kind of flaming dew that skittered along the roofs, setting fire to everything it splashed and spreading a wash of dancing flames everywhere."

LONG-RANGE MISSILES

During the war, the Germans developed jet-powered missiles. The first of these, the V-1, could fly up to 93 miles (150 km). It could be launched from France and still hit London. The next version, the V-2, was bigger and deadlier. In the United Kingdom, these weapons killed about 6,000 people. The bombs dropped by aircraft killed many more: about 43,000.

ATOMIC WEAPONS

Before the war, scientists had learned how to split atoms. Now each side raced to turn this knowledge into powerful atomic weapons. The U.S. carried out the first successful test in July 1945. They dropped two bombs on Japan the following month. The bombs killed hundreds of thousands of people.

The V-2 missile was the basis for the space rockets that were developed after the war.

EXPLOSIVE POWER OF WEAPONS COMPARED TO TONS OF TNT

Grand Slam (largest conventional bomb)
6.5 tons

Little Boy (dropped on Hiroshima)
15,000 tons

Fat Man (dropped on Nagasaki)
21,000 tons

Where Was the War Fought?

In the spring of 1940, German troops rolled through western Europe. They pushed the Allied troops back to the French coast. About 338,000 soldiers were evacuated from Dunkirk in early June. After that, there was little fighting in Western Europe until 1944. Instead, the focus of the war shifted south and east.

ITALY AND THE BALKANS

In October 1940, Italy invaded Greece, but was soon beaten back. Germany then invaded Yugoslavia before moving on to Greece. Allied forces didn't invade southern Europe until July 1943. They landed in Sicily and slowly pushed north. Mussolini was removed from power, and Italy surrendered in September.

Allied bombers pounded German positions in Italy.

HISTORY UNLOCKED

One British soldier fighting in Italy saw his friend die. He wrote this in his diary.

"With a foot blown off, he neither cried nor passed out for quite a while. One must be forced to the conclusion that he knew how he was going to take it."

INVADING THE SOVIET UNION

Hitler's agreement with the Soviet Union didn't last long. In June 1941, the German army launched a surprise attack. Hitler thought he could take the country quickly, but he was wrong. After reaching Moscow, his army was pushed back. The freezing winter and lack of supplies killed many soldiers. The battle dragged on for years. The invading army killed civilians as well as enemy troops.

FATAL FACTS

For 872 days, the Soviet city of Leningrad was surrounded by the German army. Supplies were cut off, and people began to starve. The cold winters also killed many people. About one million Soviet civilians and soldiers died during the **siege**.

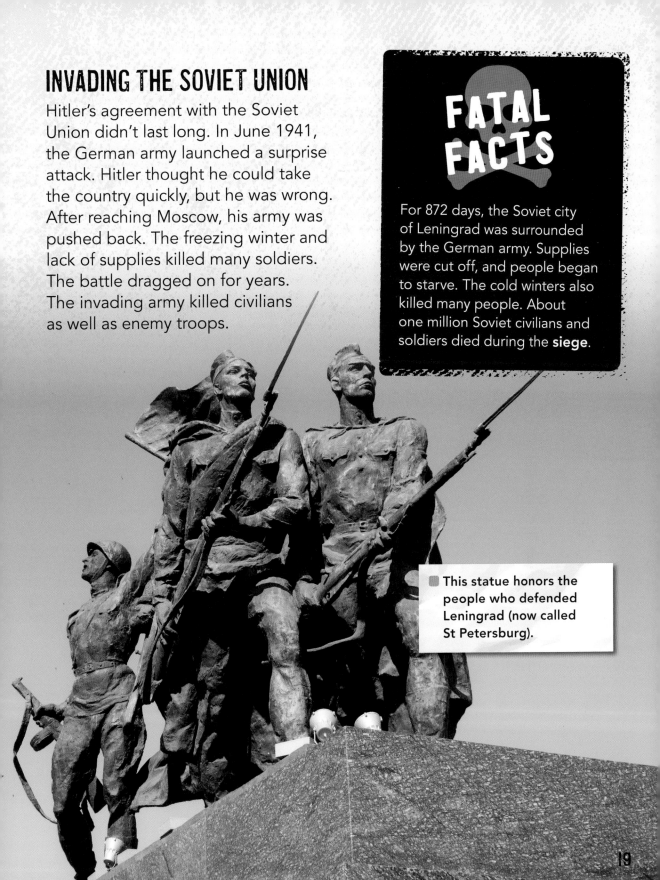

■ This statue honors the people who defended Leningrad (now called St Petersburg).

THE WAR IN THE PACIFIC

At first, the only fighting in Asia was in China. But Japan wanted to rule the entire Pacific region. Japanese forces attacked the US naval base at Pearl Harbor on December 7, 1941. The same day, they also attacked other Allied territories. Hong Kong, Malaya (now called Malaysia), and the Philippines were all invaded. The well-trained Japanese army made huge gains at first. The fighting in Southeast Asia and the Pacific was incredibly fierce.

HISTORY UNLOCKED

A U.S. Air Force pilot wrote this description of a bombing raid over the Pacific islands of Palau.

"About this time a black Zeke appeared on our left out of machine gun range. He flew there for several minutes without attempting to attack. Then the stuff hit the fan! We were attacked from all directions by Tojos and Zekes."

("Tojo" and "Zeke" were slang terms for types of Japanese fighter planes.)

■ The attack on Pearl Harbor left more than 2,400 Americans dead.

NAVAL BATTLES

Two major naval battles helped the Allies gain an edge. The Battle of the Coral Sea took place in May 1942. The U.S. Navy defeated the Japanese. This blocked their path to Australia. The next month, the U.S. Navy won the Battle of Midway. More than 3,000 Japanese troops were killed. Four of their aircraft carriers were sunk.

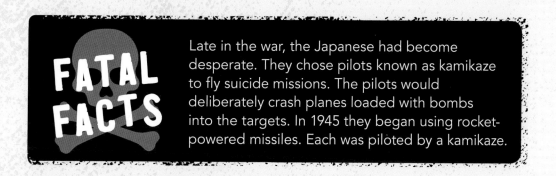

FATAL FACTS

Late in the war, the Japanese had become desperate. They chose pilots known as kamikaze to fly suicide missions. The pilots would deliberately crash planes loaded with bombs into the targets. In 1945 they began using rocket-powered missiles. Each was piloted by a kamikaze.

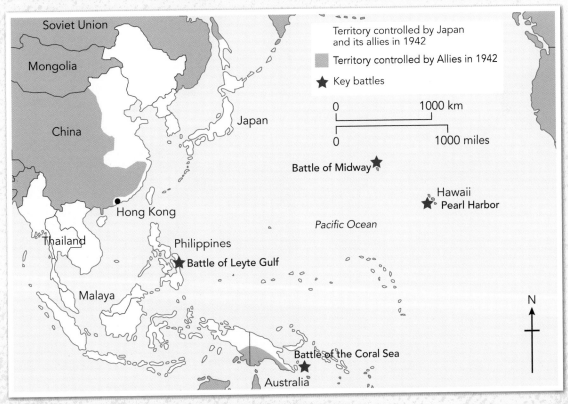

Territory controlled by Japan and its allies in 1942

Territory controlled by Allies in 1942

★ Key battles

0   1000 km

0   1000 miles

Soviet Union

Mongolia

China

Japan

Battle of Midway ★

Hawaii
★ Pearl Harbor

Hong Kong

Pacific Ocean

Thailand

Philippines

★ Battle of Leyte Gulf

Malaya

N

Battle of the Coral Sea
★

Australia

This map shows some of the main battles in the Pacific region.

AFRICA AND THE MIDDLE EAST

The Allies needed to keep control of the Suez Canal in Egypt. They used it to send supplies by sea from Europe to India and elsewhere in Asia. But British troops in Egypt were attacked by the Italians. The British won several battles. Then the Germans arrived to help the Italians. Under the command of Erwin Rommel, they pushed the British back into Egypt.

In October 1942, the two sides met in a huge tank battle at el-Alamein. Allied ships in the Mediterranean had kept supplies from reaching the Axis forces. The Allies had more tanks, more equipment, and more men. They won a decisive victory. About 14,000 soldiers on both sides were killed. Another 24,000 were wounded. 35,000 were taken prisoner.

■ Newspapers reported on the fighting in North Africa.

LA DOMENICA DEL CORRIERE

La battaglia in Egitto. Un violento attacco dell'aviazione italo-germanica distrugge e disperde un gruppo di carri armati nemici.

(Disegno di A. Beltrame)

Bernard Montgomery

Bernard Montgomery was a British general. His men affectionately called him "Monty." After taking part in the Dunkirk evacuation, he commanded British troops in North Africa. He later helped lead the Allied armies into France.

OTHER BATTLES

Italian forces had taken control of East Africa. In 1941, they were defeated by the British. There was also fighting in the Middle East. Most of this region had been under the control of European countries. Some of it still was. Some people supported the Axis, and others supported the Allies. There was bloody fighting in Iraq, Iran, Syria, Lebanon, and Palestine.

HISTORY UNLOCKED

Before el-Alamein, the British army had started using American-built Sherman tanks. These tanks were tougher and more powerful than the German tanks at the time. They carried a crew of five and had armor 4 inches (11 cm) thick.

THE BATTLE OF THE ATLANTIC

Getting supplies — such as food, weapons, troops, and raw materials — was crucial. Cutting off an enemy's supplies could really hurt them. Many of these supplies were sent by ship. The north Atlantic Ocean became a battleground. Both sides tried to keep the other's ships from getting through.

At first, British and French ships had the advantage. They were able to **blockade** Germany. But after France fell to the Nazis, the British navy struggled to cope. Ships traveled in **convoys** for protection. Military ships would escort groups of 20 to 60 commercial vessels. They would try to fight off attackers.

This American oil tanker was one of many merchant ships sunk by the enemy.

WOLF PACKS

Destroyers and other warships attacked convoys. But German **U-boats** were the biggest threat to shipping. They used a tactic called the "wolf pack." The U-boats would patrol in a long line. Once a convoy was spotted, they would converge on it. Even if some were chased or sunk by the convoy's escorts, others could still attack.

CRACKING THE CODE

The German U-boats kept in touch by radio. They used a machine called Enigma to encode their messages. They thought that the code was unbreakable, but the British managed to crack it. More importantly, they kept their success a secret. They used intercepted messages to find and attack wolf packs.

FATAL FACTS

In September 1941, a convoy of 64 merchant ships sailed from Canada to England. They were escorted by four navy ships. A wolf pack of 14 U-boats was waiting near Greenland. They sank 16 of the ships. Only about 300 sailors were killed, but important supplies were lost.

The Enigma used a combination of keys and rotors to encode messages.

THE BATTLE OF THE ATLANTIC BY THE NUMBERS

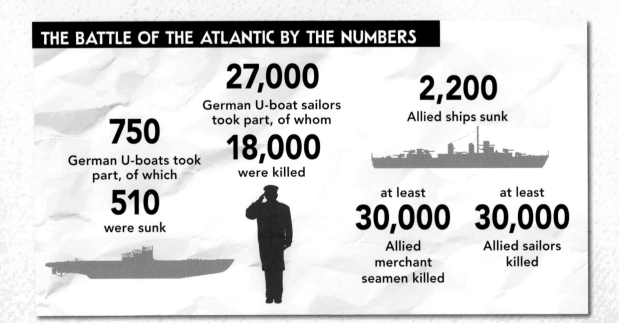

27,000
German U-boat sailors took part, of whom

750
German U-boats took part, of which

18,000
were killed

510
were sunk

2,200
Allied ships sunk

at least
30,000
Allied merchant seamen killed

at least
30,000
Allied sailors killed

Why Did So Many Civilians Die?

Everyone in the fighting nations was affected by the war. A country had to throw everything into its war effort. Factories were converted to produce weapons and uniforms. Fuel was saved for use by the armed forces. Naval blockades often kept goods and raw materials from arriving. The armed forces took priority, so people at home often had to do without.

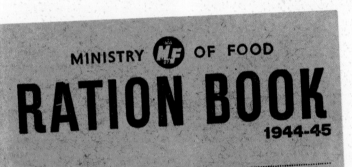

MINISTRY **MF** OF FOOD

RATION BOOK
1944-45

Surname..

Other Names..

Address..
(as on Identity Card)

Date of birth (Day)................. (Month).................

NATIONAL
REGISTRATION
NUMBER

FOOD. OFFICE CODE No.

N. D
M.F.

S.17

IF FOUND RETURN TO ANY FOOD OFFICE

HISTORY UNLOCKED

In the United Kingdom, every person was issued a **ration** book. It had coupons for foods such as eggs, sugar, and meat. When you bought food at a shop, you gave the shopkeeper some of your coupons. This way, food was shared equally. Clothes and fuel were also rationed.

THE BLITZ

Airplanes helped armies launch attacks from far away. This meant that civilians far from the front lines became targets. Starting in September 1940, German planes began dropping bombs on civilian targets in the United Kingdom. This "Blitz" lasted for eight months. About 43,000 people were killed.

Fire crews in London raced to put out fires caused by bombs.

ALLIED BOMBING RAIDS

The Allies fought back with bombing raids in Axis territory. German cities such as Hamburg, Cologne, and Düsseldorf were heavily bombed. These raids targeted factories and docks as well as residential areas. The U.S. Air Force firebombed Japanese cities, killing hundreds of thousands. Even civilians in occupied France were not safe. Many were killed as Allied bombers tried to destroy factories.

FATAL FACTS

In February 1945, Allied planes bombed Dresden, Germany. The raid lasted for three days. On the first night, 800 airplanes dropped 2,700 tons (2,450 tonnes) of bombs. Incendiary bombs started fires. The raid killed about 25,000 people.

OCCUPIED TERRITORIES

Millions of people lived in territories that were occupied by enemy forces. They tried to keep going as normal. Life could be very hard, though. In Europe, the Nazis controlled many aspects of life. Civilians could be forced to work for the Nazis. Many were killed or sent to **concentration camps**.

The Japanese occupied large parts of China and southeast Asia. In many places, they imposed **martial law**. People who didn't cooperate could be arrested, tortured, and even executed.

RESISTANCE

Secret **resistance** groups sprang up in these areas. They tried to disrupt the enemy's operations. Resistance fighters blew up railroads and damaged factories. They passed information to Allied forces. It was very dangerous, and many were caught and killed.

Hannie Schaft

Hannie Schaft was a Dutch law student. When the Nazis occupied the Netherlands, she refused to sign an oath of loyalty. She joined a resistance group. They worked to hide Jewish people and gather information. In 1945, she was captured and executed.

■ For most of the war, the Nazi flag flew over much of Europe.

INTERNMENT CAMPS

Even in free territories, civilians could be detained. Citizens of other nations were seen as a threat. In the United States, 120,000 Japanese Americans were sent to **internment camps**. They stayed there, under guard, for the rest of the war. Thousands of Germans and Italians were interned in the United Kingdom.

FATAL FACTS

Many of the people interned in the United Kingdom were sent to camps in Canada. A passenger ship on its way to Canada was was torpedoed by a German U-boat in 1940. About 800 people were killed. Many of them were **internees**.

■ Japanese Americans were forced to leave their homes.

SANTA FE TRAIL
TRANSPORTATION

LIVING IN A WAR ZONE

When troops and tanks rolled across the land, they left chaos in their wake. They destroyed buildings and took food and other supplies. Fierce battles were fought in villages, towns, and cities. In August 1942, the German army attacked Stalingrad. Soviet leaders didn't let civilians leave. They thought their army would fight harder in order to protect civilians.

The battle raged for months, and many civilians were caught up in it. Buildings were reduced to rubble as the fighting went on. About 40,000 civilians were killed. Between 1 and 2 million soldiers were killed, wounded, or captured.

■ The battle of Stalingrad lasted five months before the Germans surrendered.

REFUGEES

No one wanted to be caught in the crossfire. Others knew they would be persecuted by the invaders. Huge numbers of people left their homes, fleeing the fighting. Historians estimate that about 60 million people became **refugees** during the war. Finding food and shelter was a constant struggle.

SCORCHED EARTH

Retreating troops didn't want to leave anything that could be useful to the enemy. They often burned crops and destroyed bridges. This "scorched earth" policy made life very hard for locals. Homes were destroyed, and many people were killed. Japanese actions in China were called the "Three Alls Policy." This meant "kill all, burn all, loot all."

FATAL FACTS

Hunger probably killed more people during the war than anything else. Historians think that 20 million people starved to death. In occupied Greece, the Axis armies took food for their own use. Blockades kept supplies from arriving. Over the winter of 1941-42, about 100,000 Greeks died of starvation.

■ Starving Berliners searched for food in garbage dumps.

What War Crimes Were Committed?

The war saw terrible cruelty and suffering. Before World War II, it was accepted that this was just part of war. But the mistreatment and killing of civilians and prisoners horrified the world. Both sides had committed acts that can be considered **war crimes**. These actions ranged from mistreatment of prisoners of war (POWs) to civilian massacres and **genocide**.

PRISONERS OF WAR

The Geneva Convention was drawn up in 1929. It said that prisoners of war must be treated humanely. Their captors had to let neutral observers visit prison camps. France, Germany, the United Kingdom and the U.S. were bound by this agreement. Japan and the Soviet Union had signed it but never officially ratified it, so they were not.

■ POW camps were often crowded, but in some the prisoners were well cared for.

Millions of soldiers were taken prisoner during the war. Germany treated British, French, and American POWs fairly well. However, they treated Soviet and Polish POWs much more harshly. More than 3 million Soviet POWs died in German captivity. Many starved to death. The Soviets responded by sending hundreds of thousands of German POWs to labor camps. Most of them died.

Airey Neave

Airey Neave was a British officer captured in France in 1940. After escaping from a POW camp, he was sent to the high-security prison at Colditz. He was the first British soldier to escape from Colditz.

HISTORY UNLOCKED

Food was sometimes in short supply in POW camps. The Red Cross in the United Kingdom, Canada, and the U.S. sent more than 60 million packages to inmates. They contained food such as butter, chocolate, and powdered milk.

POWS IN ASIA

POWs held by the Japanese often received very harsh treatment. Captured Allied soldiers were beaten and forced to work as slave labor. They had little food or medical care. Tens of thousands of them died.

TARGETING CIVILIANS

In World War II, civilians were in the firing line. Both sides killed people who were seen as expendable. Some military leaders thought targeting civilians would hurt morale. Others thought that their enemies were inferior and deserved to die. Bombs killed hundreds of thousands. There were also other ways of targeting civilians.

FORCED LABOR

In occupied Poland, all men were forced to do unpaid labor. They worked in factories, built railroads, and dug tunnels. Working conditions were often dangerous. Many sites were targeted by Allied bombers. In Asia, millions of Chinese civilians were forced to work for the Japanese.

■ The Japanese used Chinese workers to help re-open an important road.

MASSACRES

Some of the most horrifying events were massacres. Hundreds or even thousands of people would be killed in one brutal attack. In 1937, Japanese troops took control of Nanjing, China. They rampaged through the streets. Between 100,000 and 300,000 civilians were killed. In Russia, Soviet soldiers took more than 4,400 Polish officers into the Katyn forest and executed them.

FATAL FACTS

The resistance was causing trouble in occupied France. The Nazis wanted revenge. They rounded up everyone in the village of Oradour-sur-Glane. They locked them in buildings, then set them on fire. 190 men, 245 women, and 207 children died. Only 10 survived.

Nazi troops massacred the people of the Czech village of Lidice. It was revenge for the assassination of a high-ranking Nazi, even though the villagers had nothing to do with it.

THE HOLOCAUST

Hitler and the Nazis hated the Jewish people. They thought that Jewish people were responsible for Germany's problems. Even before the war, Jewish people in Germany were persecuted. Once the war started, the Nazis took it further. They began to make plans for getting rid of all of the Jewish people in Europe. They called this the "Final Solution."

Wherever the German army went, they rounded up Jewish people. Some were killed right away, and some were sent to live in crowded **ghettos**. Others were used as slave labor. They were given little food and worked until they collapsed.

■ These Jewish women are being led into the woods to be shot.

CONCENTRATION CAMPS

Hitler sent special troops to kill Jewish people in occupied territories. These groups probably killed about 1 million people. However, it wasn't efficient enough for the Nazis. They started sending Jewish people to concentration camps, such as Auschwitz. Men, women, and children would be forced onto crowded freight trains. Once they arrived, some would be selected to work as slaves. Others were sent directly to gas chambers, where they were killed with poison gas. Their bodies were then burned.

OTHER VICTIMS

Jewish people were the main victims, but other groups suffered too. Polish and Romani people died in concentration camps. So did thousands of homosexuals and disabled people. The Nazis also targeted those with political ideas that they didn't like. Millions of people were killed.

Many inmates in concentration camps starved to death.

COUNTRIES THAT LOST MOST OF THEIR JEWISH POPULATION DURING THE HOLOCAUST

Country	Percentage
Hungary	69%
Netherlands	71%
Latvia	78%
Lithuania	85%
Greece	86%
Poland	90%

How Did the War End?

The Axis powers made huge gains early in the war. But when the United States entered the war, it was a big boost to the Allies. They provided much-needed troops and equipment. In late 1942, after some key Allied victories, the tide began to turn. Italy surrendered in September 1943.

PROBLEMS FOR THE AXIS

The Germans were running low on men and equipment. Blockades kept food and raw materials from getting through. Factories were hit by Allied bombing raids. Even worse, the invasion of the Soviet Union had gone horribly wrong. German troops were being pushed back. In the Pacific, Japan didn't have the resources to keep control of the lands they had captured. The U.S. Navy had destroyed much of their fleet.

Victory by U.S. troops in the Battle of Leyte in 1944 was the first step toward re-taking the Philippines.

D-DAY

Bombing raids had caused real damage in occupied Europe. Now the Allies thought the time was right for an invasion. On June 6, 1944, Allied soldiers landed in northern France. About 7,000 ships set sail from England. They landed 133,000 soldiers on the beaches.

The Germans fought back, but it was the beginning of the end. By the end of June, 850,000 Allied soldiers and 150,000 vehicles had arrived in France. In the east, Soviet troops were making gains. Hitler's days were numbered.

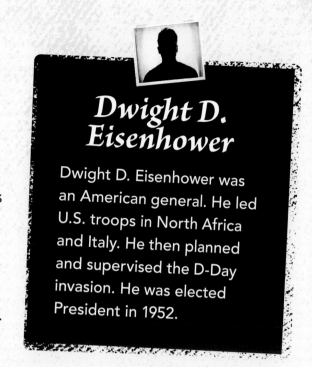

Dwight D. Eisenhower

Dwight D. Eisenhower was an American general. He led U.S. troops in North Africa and Italy. He then planned and supervised the D-Day invasion. He was elected President in 1952.

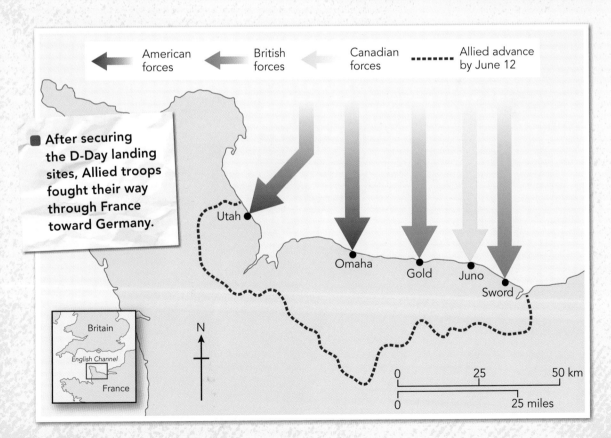

American forces

British forces

Canadian forces

Allied advance by June 12

After securing the D-Day landing sites, Allied troops fought their way through France toward Germany.

Utah

Omaha

Gold

Juno

Sword

Britain

English Channel

France

N

0   25   50 km

0   25 miles

THE FALL OF BERLIN

By late 1944, Allied armies were closing in on Germany. Hitler launched one last, desperate attack in Belgium in December. The Allies managed to push back the German troops. Soviet soldiers reached Berlin in April. They pounded it with shells and fought their way in. On April 30, Hitler committed suicide. His deputies surrendered, and on May 8, the war in Europe was over.

Victorious Soviet soldiers raised their flag over Berlin.

WAR IN THE PACIFIC

However, fighting in the Pacific still raged. The Japanese armed forces had been weakened. American bombers destroyed towns and industrial sites. Ground troops slowly pushed their way forward. About 20,000 Japanese soldiers died defending the island of Iwo Jima. Some killed themselves rather than surrender.

ENDING THE WAR

The Allies did not want to have to invade Japan. Previous battles had cost many lives on both sides. The Japanese had shown that they would not give up, but would keep fighting. However, the United States had a powerful new weapon: atomic bombs. Using them against Japan would kill hundreds of thousands of civilians. But they might end the war, preventing a long and bloody invasion. U.S. President Harry Truman decided to use them. The cities of Hiroshima and Nagasaki were bombed in August. A week later, Japan surrendered.

More than half the buildings in Hiroshima were destroyed in the bombing.

HIROSHIMA AND NAGASAKI BOMBINGS BY THE NUMBERS

	Hiroshima	Nagasaki
Population before bombing	255,000	195,000
Size of bomb	4.9 tons	5.4 tons
People killed immediately	80,000	40,000
Total death toll	135,000	64,000

What Were the Effects of the War?

The war was over, but the world was in chaos. Tens of millions of people had died. Just as many were now refugees, trying to find a way home. Cities and towns had been reduced to rubble. Food was scarce. In many places, there was no real authority. Violence and looting were common.

After the war, people in occupied countries who had cooperated with the Nazis were publicly shamed.

JUSTICE FOR THE VICTIMS

Many people wanted revenge for what had happened. The Holocaust and other acts were classified as war crimes. Hundreds of German and Japanese leaders and soldiers were tried and executed. A few Allied soldiers were also tried for committing war crimes.

Top Nazis such as Hermann Goering (center) were tried and sentenced to death.

PREVENTING ANOTHER WAR

Everyone agreed that another world war must never happen. World leaders founded the United Nations in October 1945. This organization tries to maintain peace and settle disputes between nations. They have even sent peacekeeping troops to conflict areas.

A NEW WORLD ORDER

The United States and the Soviet Union were now the world's main superpowers. They had been allies, but they were radically different. The US was based on **capitalism** and democracy. The Soviet Union was **communist**. Their clash of ideals shaped the next few decades.

Timeline

1933–1938

January 30, 1933	Adolf Hitler becomes Chancellor of Germany.
July 7, 1937	Japan invades China.
March 13, 1938	Germany takes control of Austria.
September 29, 1938	Germany, France, Italy, and the United Kingdom sign the Munich Agreement.

1939

August 23	Germany and the Soviet Union sign a secret agreement not to go to war.
September 1	Germany invades Poland.
September 3	France and the United Kingdom declare war on Germany.

1940

April 9	Germany invades Denmark and Norway.
May 10	Germany invades Belgium, the Netherlands, and Luxembourg. Winston Churchill becomes prime minister of the United Kingdom.
May 26–June 3	British and French troops are evacuated from Dunkirk, France.
June 22	France and Germany sign an armistice.
July–October	Germany conducts bombing raids on military and industrial targets in the United Kingdom.

1941

Sept 1940–May 1941	German bombers attack civilian targets in Britain.
22 June 22	Germany invades the Soviet Union.
September 8	Leningrad is cut off by the German army and a siege begins.
December 7	Japan attacks the U.S. naval base at Pearl Harbor, Hawaii.
December 8	The U.S. and United Kingdom declare war on Japan.

1942

May 4–8	The Battle of the Coral Sea repels a Japanese invasion.
June 6	The Battle of Midway ends in a U.S. victory over Japan.
November 6	The Allies win the Battle of el-Alamein in North Africa.

1943

January 31	The Battle of Stalingrad ends with a German surrender.
September 8	Italy surrenders and leaves the war.

1944

January 27	The siege of Leningrad finally ends.
June 6	D-Day: Allied troops invade northern France.
August 25	Paris is liberated from German control.
October 20	U.S. troops invade the Philippines.
October 23–26	The Battle of Leyte Gulf ends with an Allied victory.
December 16	The Battle of the Bulge (Germany's last major offensive) begins.

1945

February 13–15	Allied planes firebomb Dresden, Germany.
March 9–10	The U.S. firebombs Tokyo.
April 22	Soviet troops enter Berlin.
April 30	Hitler commits suicide.
May 8	Germany surrenders, and the war in Europe is over.
August 6	The U.S. drops an atomic bomb on Hiroshima, Japan.
August 9	A second atomic bomb is dropped on the Japanese city of Nagasaki.
August 15	Japan surrenders and the war ends.
October 24	The United Nations organization begins operation.

GLOSSARY

ammunition (am-yuh-NI-shuhn)—bullets and other objects that can be fired from weapons

artillery (ar-TI-luhr-ee)—cannons and other large guns used during battles

atomic bomb (uh-TOM-ik BOM)—a powerful bomb that explodes with great force and leaves behind dangerous radiation

blockade (blok-AYD)—a closing off of an area to keep people or supplies from going in or out

capitalism (CAP-it-ul-i-zuhm)—economic system that allows people to create businesses and own as much property as they can afford

chancellor (CHAN-suh-luhr)—a title for the leader of a country

civilian (si-VIL-yuhn)—a person who is not in the military

communism (KAHM-yuh-ni-zuhm)—a way of organizing a country so that all the land, houses, and factories belong to the government, and the profits are shared by all

compensation (com-pen-SAY-shun)—money paid in recognition of loss or suffering

concentration camp (kahn-suhn-TRAY-shuhn KAMP)—a prison camp where thousands of inmates are held under harsh conditions

convoy (KAHN-voy)—a protective escort of ships or boats

democracy (di-MAH-kruh-see)—a form of government in which the citizens can choose their leaders

depression (di-PRE-shuhn)—a period during which business, jobs, and stock values stay low

dictator (DIK-tay-tuhr)—someone who has complete control of a country

fascism (FASH-i-zuhm)—right-wing form of government with extreme nationalistic ideals

firebomb (FYR BAHM)—to target with incendiary bombs

genocide (JEN-oh-side)—to destroy a race of people on purpose

ghetto (GET-oh)—a poor neighborhood in a city where people of the same race live

incendiary bomb (in-SEND-ee-air-ee BAHM)—bomb that is filled with flammable material, designed to start fires

inflation (in-FLAY-shuhn)—an increase in prices

internee (in-tuhr-NEE)—person detained in an internment camp

internment camp (in-TERN-ment KAMP)—place where citizens are detained because they are seen to be a danger during war

martial law (MAR-shul LAW)—control of a people by the government's military, instead of by civilian forces, often during an emergency

neutral (NOO-truhl)—not taking any side in a war

propaganda (PROP-uh-GAN-duh)—information spread to try to influence the thinking of people

primary source (PRYE-mair-ee SORSS)—source from someone who experienced an event firsthand

ration (RASH-uhn)—limit on an item intented to ensure that it doesn't run out

refugee (ref-yuh-JEE)—a person forced to flee his or her home because of natural disaster or war

resistance (ri-ZISS-tuhnss)—secret organization resisting authority in an occupied country

siege (SEEJ)—an attack designed to surround a place and cut it off from supplies or help

tactic (TAK-tik)—a plan for fighting a battle

torpedo (tor-PEE-doh)—an underwater missile

U-boat (YOU BOTE)—a German submarine

war crime (WAR KRYM)—act that violates the accepted international rules of war

READ MORE

Books

Biskup, Agnieszka. *D-Day*. 24-Hour History. Chicago: Raintree, 2015.

Marriott, Emma. *Did Anything Good Come Out of World War II? Innovation Through Adversity*. New York: Rosen Publishing, 2016.

Servin, Morgan. *World War II Close Up*. The War Chronicles. New York: Rosen Publishing, 2016.

Stein, R. Conrad. *World War II in the Pacific: From Pearl Harbor to Nagasaki*. The United States at War. New York: Enslow Publishing, 2011.

Throp, Claire. *Resisting the Nazis*. Heroes of World War II. Chicago: Raintree, 2016.

Internet Sites

FactHound offers a safe, fun way to find Internet sites related to this book. All of the sites on FactHound have been researched by our staff.

Here's all you do:

Visit *www.facthound.com*

Type in this code: 9781484841651

Places to Visit

Museum of Science and Industry
5700 S. Lake Shore Drive
Chicago, IL 60637
https://www.msichicago.org

National Museum of American History
Constitution Avenue, NW
Washington, D.C. 20001
http://americanhistory.si.edu

National World War II Memorial
900 Ohio Drive SW
Washington, D.C. 20024
https://www.nps.gov/wwii/index.htm

Critical Thinking Questions

Which parts of this book did you find the most interesting? What subjects would you like to know more about?

How did the end of World War I set the stage for World War II?

Describe how life for civilians in occupied territories was different from life for civilians away from the front lines. Support your answer using information from at least two other texts or valid Internet sources.

In what ways were civilians targeted? Why were both sides willing to target civilians? Support your answer using information from at least two other texts or valid Internet resources.

INDEX